Bourbon Tails

By Beth Andrews

Photography: Beth Andrews
Design: Hill Harcourt/Ashton Advertising
Cartoons: Rick Maynard www.rickmaynard.com

Pictured on the front cover: Red
Pictured on the back cover: LuLu

ISBN: 978-1-61850-161-5

Text and photographs copyright ©2022 Bourbon Tails

Printed by Tailored Group LLC. All rights reserved. No portion of this book may be reproduced, stored in a retrieval system or transmitted in any form or by any means, mechanical, electronic, photocopying, recording, or otherwise, without written permission from the photographer. Excerpts may be used for promotional or review purposes.

Third Printing
Printed and bound in The United States
Printed through Tailored Group LLC, Louisville, KY

bourbontails.com

PHOTOGRAPHER BETH ANDREWS

The first hint of "Bourbon Tails" drifted into in my mind one warm summer evening at my brother John's small farm. He was throwing a stick for his dog and drinking a bourbon as the sun was setting over the bluegrass-covered hill and quiet pond. I thought to myself that it was a perfect Kentucky moment.

Dogs and horses have been an integral part of my life since I can remember. That's the reason my career took the unconventional path of animal photography after many years in broadcasting as an anchor/reporter and meteorologist, and a few years in guest services and development. As a photographer, I have the ability to turn a fleeting moment into permanence. In this book, I have the opportunity to make permanent a fleeting thought, and to share it with all of you who love dogs and appreciate a good bourbon!

I hope you will enjoy these dogs as much as I enjoyed photographing them and meeting their people. As a longtime Board member for the Kentucky Humane Society, I am dedicated to using a significant part of the proceeds from this book to help this great organization make every Kentucky dog a happy dog.

Thanks to all the incredible people who brought their dogs out to the distilleries in all kinds of weather. Dogs and distilleries are a beautiful combination. Some of the distillery executives even flew their dogs in for the shoots. It deeply warms my heart to see the excitement everyone has about this book, and their dedication to making it a success.

Most importantly, thank you to my family. My parents gave us an animated childhood with family dogs, cats, horses, bunnies, ducks and, at one point, a peculiarly affectionate bull named Tex. My husband Bruce is the smartest person I know and my biggest fan; my stepdaughter Andrea is deeply kind and a light wherever she goes; and my son Jake inspires me with his own love for animals and dedication to making the world a better place for them.

Of course, my family is terribly incomplete without my two sweet horses and my silly little adopted dogs, Tater Tot and Dottie Jane. Like a fine bourbon distiller, I'm putting much love and care into my dogs' maturation and, in return, they make my life 100 proof every single day.

PENNY

John and Tina Schaaf

Photographed at Kentucky Artisan Distillery

Penny has quite the dog's life on her farm. She is a great family dog and makes it her mission to keep up with all members of the household. She even knows what order everyone gets up in the morning and she pouts if she doesn't get to wake everyone up separately.

Favorite Activity: Playing with balls, sticks and frisbees
Best Skill: Fetching in the lake
Favorite Treats: Dairy Queen and Pup Cups
Pet Peeve: Skunks

ALPHA

Wes Henderson, Co-Founder and Chief Innovation Officer of Angel's Envy Distillery

Alpha is strong, protective and loving. He is one of four dogs in the Henderson household but he is, quite predictably, the Alpha.

Best Trick: Talking

Favorite Activity: Catching turtles and depositing them, alive and well, in the house

SOOKIE

John Wadell, Single Barrel Curator, at Kentucky Peerless Distilling Company

Sookie started her life with John after he visited the Kentucky Humane Society. Now she keeps him entertained with her silliness and her loving personality.

Favorite things: Tennis balls and big dogs

Favorite Treat: Nylabones, but not to eat. She only likes hiding them in shoeboxes and pillowcases

Pet Peeves: Pot holders and the Swiffer Wet Jet or anything else that rolls.

ALLY

Ryan Babb, Maintenance Manager at Michter's Distillery

Ally was adopted from the Kentucky Humane Society and loves to watch movies, her favorite being Star Wars. She's not picky about which episode but prefers the ones that feature the Death Star and Storm Troopers, since those are her favorite toys!

Favorite Treat: Chewies

Best Friends: Brinkly and Daisy

CHICO

Cathy Shircliff

Photographed at The Woodford Reserve Distillery

Chico is the sweetest and most loving boy. He is happiest when he's with his family and loves nothing more than a "family night in," chilling on the bed and getting scratches!

Favorite Food: Cheese and corn on the cob

Greatest Skill: His bear-like ability to find and acquire snacks. He's even pulled down a table runner to achieve his goals.

Favorite Activity: Wading like a hippo in water up to his belly

WATSON

Katie Farley, VIP/Trade/Media Manager at The Woodford Reserve Distillery

Watson is quite the character, and most popular everywhere he goes. While he may seem like he's the man in charge, he sometimes shows his inner chicken. He is even terrified in his own house when things are out of place.

Nickname: Puppy Dog
Best Trick: Fist bumping to the command "Pound it"
Favorite Spot: Snuggled up to Katie's legs for a good nap
Favorite Treat: Carrots

WINNIE

Katie Farley, VIP/Trade/ Media Manager at The Woodford Reserve Distillery

Winnie is an adorable ball of joy. She is fearless and playful and is a true "bull dog in a china shop"! She has a little hitch in her step, due to a broken leg when she was little, but that makes her even cuter and hasn't slowed her down one bit.

Often found: Doing "zoomies"

Favorite Activity: Playing with the baby horses

Favorite Treat: Bananas

WATSON and WINNIE
Photographed at The Woodford Reserve Distillery

FINN

Andrew and Christa Lueken
Photographed at Maker's Mark Distillery

Trouble often comes in tiny packages. Finn is an undisputed force of nature. He's one of three Doxies so he must think he has to work a little harder to make his presence known. He always carries out his naughty antics with a ready smile, which endears him to everyone!

Favorite Pastime: Destroying "non-destructible" toys

Favorite treat: Anything in the garbage can

Pet Peeve: Moles, which is why he must dig endless craters in the yard

FINN
Photographed at Maker's Mark Distillery

Paws for Thought...

If you want to call your bourbon "straight bourbon," you have to age it for at least two years in the barrel. If you age it less than four years, you have to put an age statement somewhere on the bottle telling folks just how long you aged it.

"The good news is that this is the finest Kentucky Bourbon. The bad news is that it still has two years to age."

BEASLEY and ELIZABETH MCCALL

Elizabeth McCall, Assistant Master Distiller for The Woodford Reserve Distillery

Beasley found his way to Elizabeth through a local rescue organization and he immediately melted her heart with his soulful eyes and adorable face. Beasley loves morning walks and trips to the farm, where he zooms around and finds water to splash in and balls to carry. He showers his family with so much love they would be completely lost without him.

Favorite Activity: Playing fetch and stuffing as many balls as possible in his mouth at once

Best Talent: Burying bones and covering the holes so well they look untouched

Can Often Be Found: Posing as Superman on the ground

The Woodford Woof Punch

Pitcher recipe:
6 cups sun tea
3 cups strawberry lemonade
3 cups orange juice
4 cups Woodford Reserve Distillery Select Bourbon

Cocktail recipe:
3 oz. sun tea
1.5 oz. strawberry lemonade
1.5 oz. orange juice
2 oz. Woodford Reserve Distillery Select Bourbon

For both:
Pour over ice and garnish with mint.

BEASLEY

Photographed at The Woodford Reserve Distillery

BOBBY

Michelle and Aaron Tasman

Photographed at Rabbit Hole Distillery

Bobby is the sweetest, happiest dog ever. He is incomplete when his family is not showering him with love. He considers himself to be the fourth child!

Favorite Foods: Anything that comes off his "siblings'" plates

Usually Found: Begging for a tummy scratch

Full Name: Bobby Hans Twinkle Toes

BOO

Jaclyn Poore

Photographed at Jeptha Creed Distillery

Boo is a silly little dog with a big personality. When he's not posing for photographs, he's playing tennis or frantically trying to get rubs. He'll do just about anything to get attention, but with that sweet face and intense gaze, he really doesn't have to do much!

Often Found: Dragging something, usually his bed

Favorite Place: Under the covers

MADI

Michelle Ragland, Accountant at Brown-Forman
Photographed at Early Times Distillery

Madi is a happy girl who is known for her sweetness and kind heart. She's friendly to everyone and loves to go places with her mom-especially if it involves riding in a golf cart!

Favorite Snacks: Cheez-Its

Favorite Activity: Chasing deer on TV

WOLFIE

Joyce Netherly, Co-Owner and Master Distiller at Jeptha Creed Distillery

Joyce found little Wolfie on the side of the road. He ran under a truck but somehow was not hit, and he jumped into her arms where he is still found most of the time. Now he has the very important and demanding job of being official greeter at Jeptha Creed. With a personality to match his adorable appearance, he is a hit with all the guests!

Favorite Activity: Giving kisses

Best Friend: Bourbon the Labrador

Pet Peeve: Water bottles

WOLFIE
Photographed at Jeptha Creed Distillery

BARLEY

Brent Elliott, Master Distiller at Four Roses Distillery

Brent fondly describes Barley as a wonderful dog whose heart is as big as the world and whose brain is as small as a speck of dust. She seems equally excited and confused by the events of her day, but she is happy and silly and much loved. Her name, Barley, comes from one of the main ingredients in bourbon!

Favorite Treat: Bacon

Favorite Activity: Running in circles

Best Trick: Growls for attention

BOOZIE
Photographed at Maker's Mark Distillery

BOOZIE

Kathy and Sam Cook

Photographed at Maker's Mark Distillery

Boozie was supposed to be named Maker's, but his littermate Mark wasn't ready to go home so Boozie ended up being the only pup in the Cook house. They named him while toasting Sam's dad with a glass of Maker's Mark.

Favorite Activity: Boat rides and walks

Favorite Treats: Kroger bags because they contain infinite treats and toys

BRANDY

Autumn Netherly, Co-owner and Marketing Manager at Jeptha Creed Distillery

Brandy loves "Bring Your Dog to Work Day" at Jeptha Creed Distillery, which is most of the time. She is always joined by her buddy Wolfie, and sometimes by other dogs. Jeptha Creed has an invisible fence around their distillery so that dogs can come to their Friday Night Concerts. Sometimes they even have adoptable dogs there for people to meet. It is one dog-friendly distillery!

Favorite Treat: Lettuce

Favorite Activity: Chasing moles and, unfortunately, skunks

The Pink Hound

2 oz. Jeptha Creed bourbon
1.5 oz. grapefruit juice
.5 oz. lemon juice
.5 oz. simple syrup
2 dashes bitters
1 egg white (optional)

Shake vigorously with ice. Strain into a rocks glass with ice. Garnish with an orange slice.

TATER TOT

Beth Andrews and Bruce Perkins. Photographed at Michter's Distillery

Tater Tot was an impulse adoption from the Kentucky Humane Society. He was born with such an innocent and adorable appearance that he escapes blame for endless mischievous escapades. While his family often calls him "14 pounds of terror", this little terrier is the sweetest and cuddliest boy on the planet and wins the hearts of everyone he encounters.

Nickname: Tiny Bubbles

Favorite Activity: Eating. At mealtime he will run around the kitchen grabbing and shaking all the kitchen towels and biting the appliances until his little mouth is filled with food.

Usually Found: Snuggling in a lap or in bed.

Pet Peeve: Vacuums

Favorite Treats: Peanut butter cookies and watermelon

LEON and GUS

John and Patti Rhea
John is Former COO and Patti is Distillery Lab Manager of Four Roses Distillery

Leon and Gus are super happy and loyal dogs. They follow their parents around everywhere and are just happy to be with them!

LEON

Usually Found: Under the coffee table

Weirdest Trick: Chewing rocks and presenting them as prizes

Pet Peeve: Being told he's not a couch dog

GUS

Favorite Activity: Playing football and baseball with humans

Most Endearing Trait: He loves to hold hands

Pet Peeves: Box fans and deer

Paws for Thought...
To be considered bourbon, the distillate must be aged in a new charred oak barrel. Most often these barrels are white oak, but they can be any variety of oak.

If it comes out of a white oak barrel, it's perfect.

Coach is photographed outside one of the doghouses built at the Early Times Distillery. The distillery pays for the training of service dogs and the houses go with the dogs to their forever homes.

COACH

Michael Stull, Plant Production Leader at Brown-Forman
Photographed at Early Times Distillery

Coach is named after Coach Gene Keady of Purdue. Not surprisingly, he can often be found wearing his football jersey and bumming hot dogs at Purdue tailgates. He enjoys most tailgate food, but is most pleased when the rare pork chop comes his way.

Favorite Activity: Walking to restaurants
Favorite Place: In the center of everything
Pet Peeve: The Rumba Vacuum

DAISY

Ryan Ashley, COO and Director of Distillery Operations at Four Roses Distillery

Daisy was rescued from a hoarder when she was a puppy. She seems to demonstrate her gratitude every day with kisses and affection. Daisy uses her brindle coloring to be a stealth stalker of all the varmints in the yard, her favorite being the elusive mole. She also has a keen mothering instinct and has even cared for newborn kittens.

Usually Found: Trying to please her people

Pet Peeve: The doorbell – she will use whatever person she is cuddling with at the time to launch herself across the room to the door

Favorite Place: In the bed, where she settles into one spot and never moves

DAISY
Photographed at Four Roses Distillery

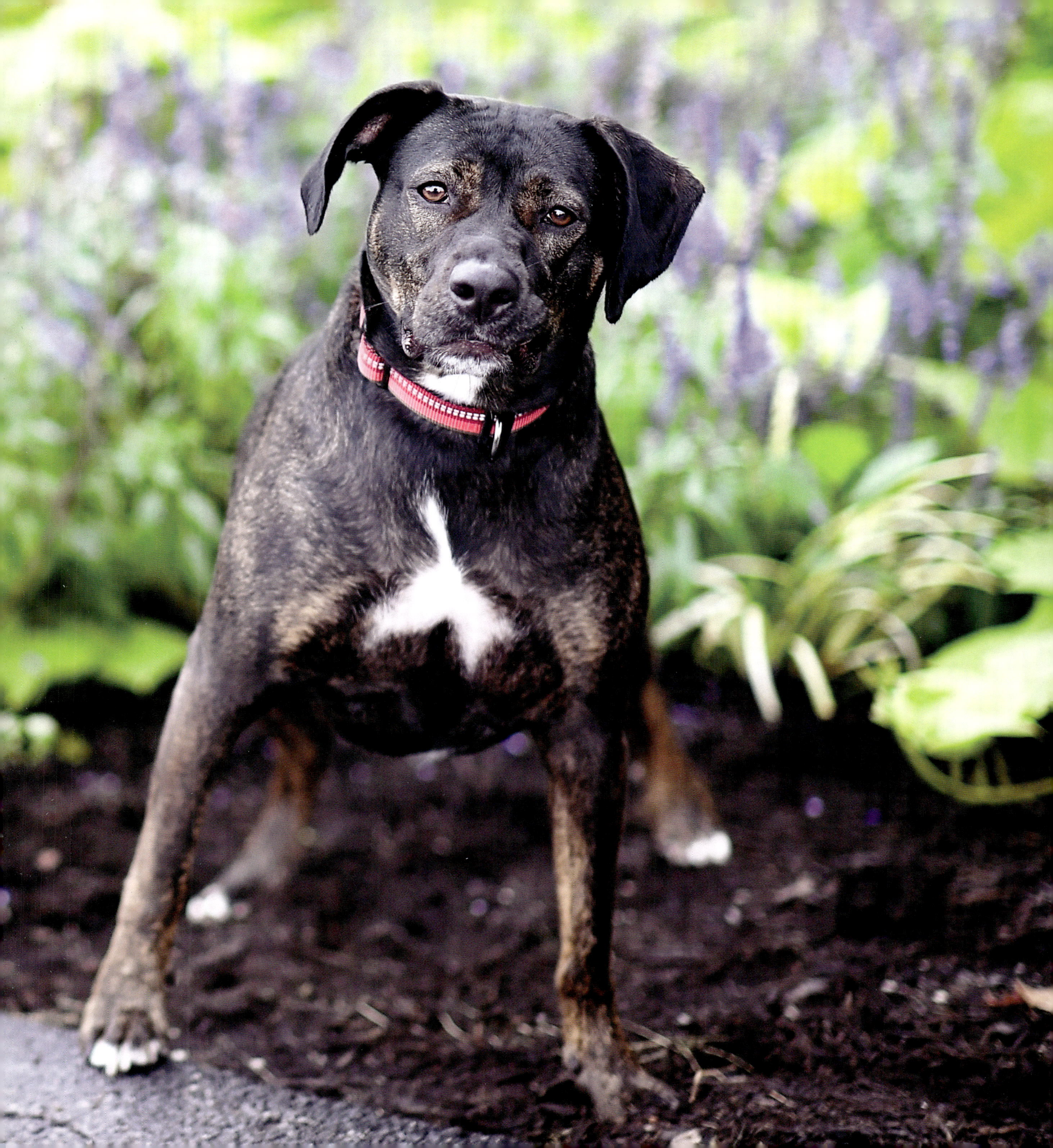

FILLY

Jim Hoerner, Operator at Brown-Forman
Photographed at Early Times Distillery

You might think Filly got her name because she's, well, as big as a small horse.
But actually, it is because she was surrendered to the Kentucky Humane Society on Oaks Day.
She landed in a wonderful place with her dad Jim.

Best Trick: Barking at her neighbor's house until the neighbor appears with a peanut butter treat

Favorite Snack: Obviously… peanut butter

Favorite Activity: Watching basketball on TV and following the ball

DIAMOND

Marjorie Amon, Visitor Center Manager at James E. Pepper Distillery

Diamond is a lively boy who grew up on a farm but is adjusting to city life just fine! He is sweet to everyone and frequently smiles at people- sometimes so hard that he has to sneeze.

Most Endearing Trait: He stares deeply into people's eyes

Most Distinctive Feature: The diamond on his head that gave him his name

Pet Peeve: Storms

DIXIE with JULIAN P. VAN WINKLE III

Dixie came from the Kentucky Humane Society and has a strong resemblance to Thunder, the dog on the bottle of 20-year Pappy Van Winkle Family Reserve! She's very friendly and loves everyone she meets.

Favorite Activity: Following her nose wherever it takes her
Best Talent: Fetching…when she feels like it

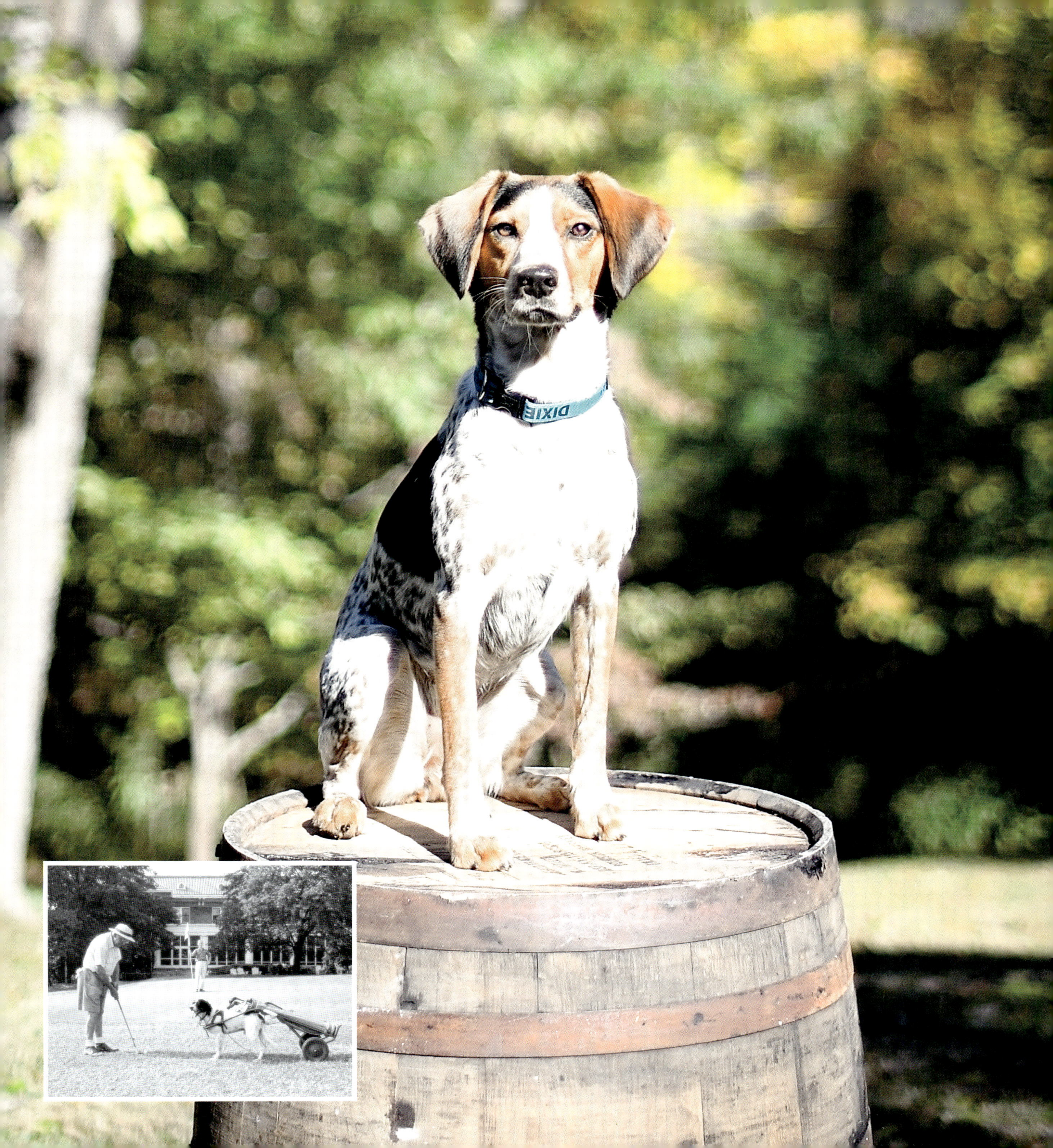
DIXIE

EZRA and BAILEY

Shaun Wilson, Creative Marketing at Kentucky Peerless Distilling Company

Ezra and Bailey are brothers and best friends. They were born during an ice storm on Valentine's Day in 2011. Bailey is a lover and a socialite; Ezra is a Tasmanian devil who prefers running to socializing. They are both very cuddly and affectionate and always ready for their next adventure.

Favorite Place: Red River Gorge

Often Found: Riding on their boat

ALLY

Photographed at Michter's Distillery

DOTTIE JANE

Beth Andrews and Bruce Perkins
Photographed at Michter's Distillery

Dottie Jane came to the Kentucky Humane Society from a small overcrowded shelter in Eastern Kentucky. She was nursing puppies even though she was only a year old. She and her babies were all adopted, and through living a carefree life, she has discovered her true self: a silly, sweet and very loving little girl.

Greatest Talents: Fancy dancing and yoga stretches

Usually found: In the living room chair- now named the "Queen's Chair"

Pet Peeve: Walking bridges

Favorite Pastime: Kisses and hugs

WHISKEY WILLIAM

Navy Keeling, First Shift Support Utility at Heaven Hill Distillery

Whiskey William is an adorable little guy who wants to constantly be the center of attention. He would rather be in someone's lap than anyplace else on the planet!

Favorite Toy: ALL the toys!! Preferably piled on the couch

Best Trick: Dancing for treats

Paws for Thought...

Small batch bourbon is bourbon produced by mixing the contents of a relatively small number of selected barrels. Single barrel bourbon is a higher grade of bourbon that comes from an individual barrel.

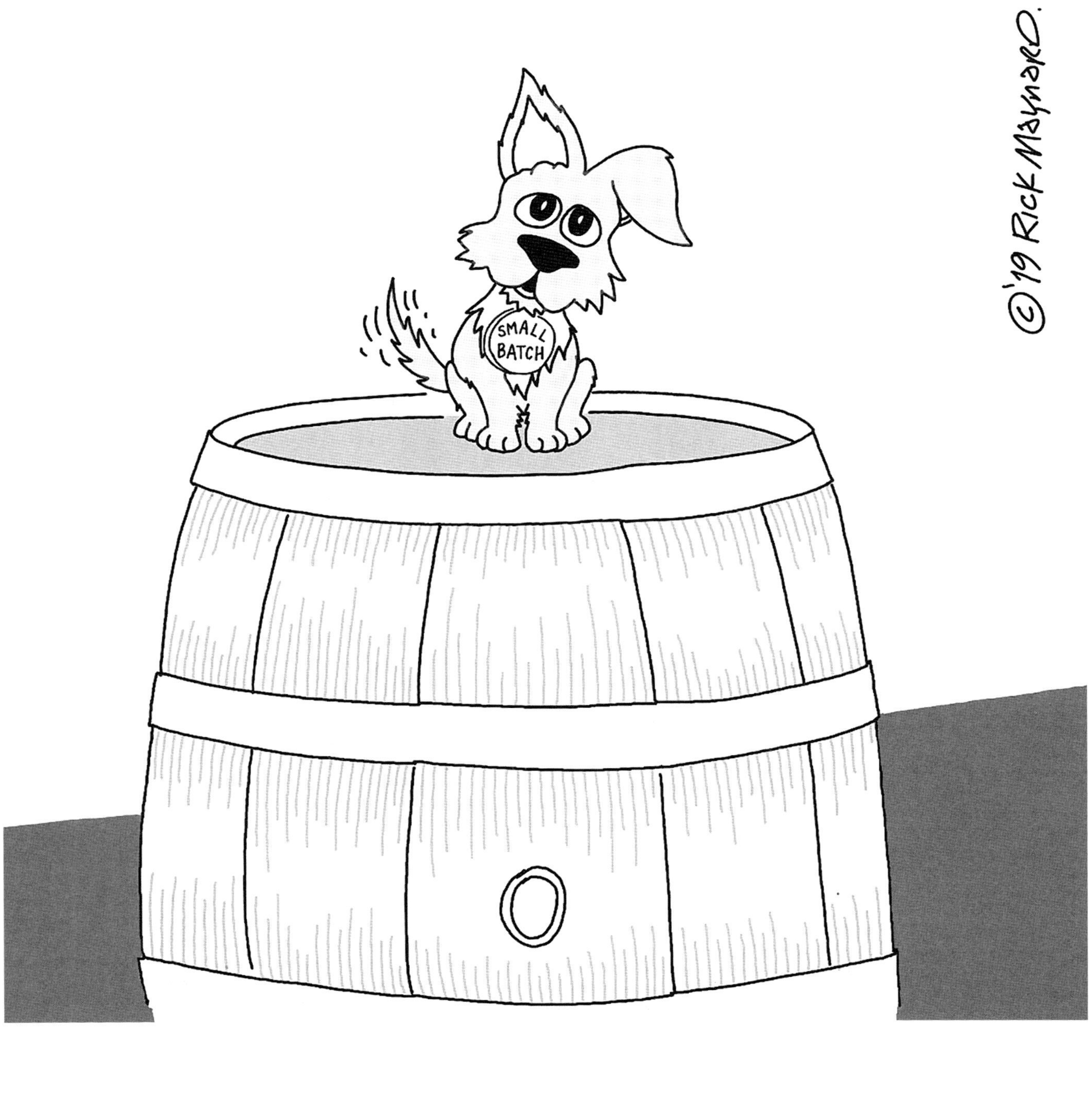
SMALL BATCH
©'19 RICK MAYNARD

FRANKLIN

Vicky Fugitte, Visitor Experience Manager at Michter's Distillery

Franklin is a sweet little guy who loves road trips, swimming in the lake and piano music. He also enjoys a good nap, as long as he can sleep under covers with his head on a pillow.

Best Friend: Buddy the Guinea Pig
Favorite Toy: His hedgehog
Favorite Snack: Chicken Nuggets

GUINNESS WAYNE

Kelsey Shannon, Assistant Communications Manager at Heaven Hill Distillery

Guinness is proclaimed to be the world's biggest cuddler! Every day is happy when you are in his world. With such a natural skill at cuddling, it was important they buy a California King bed so that he could properly fit and therefore achieve his full cuddling potential. He is not spoiled at all!

Favorite Place: In bed (of course)

Best Trick: High Jumping

Best Trick he refuses to perform: Staying. He knows how to do it but respectfully declines.

FRANKLIN

Photographed at Michter's Distillery

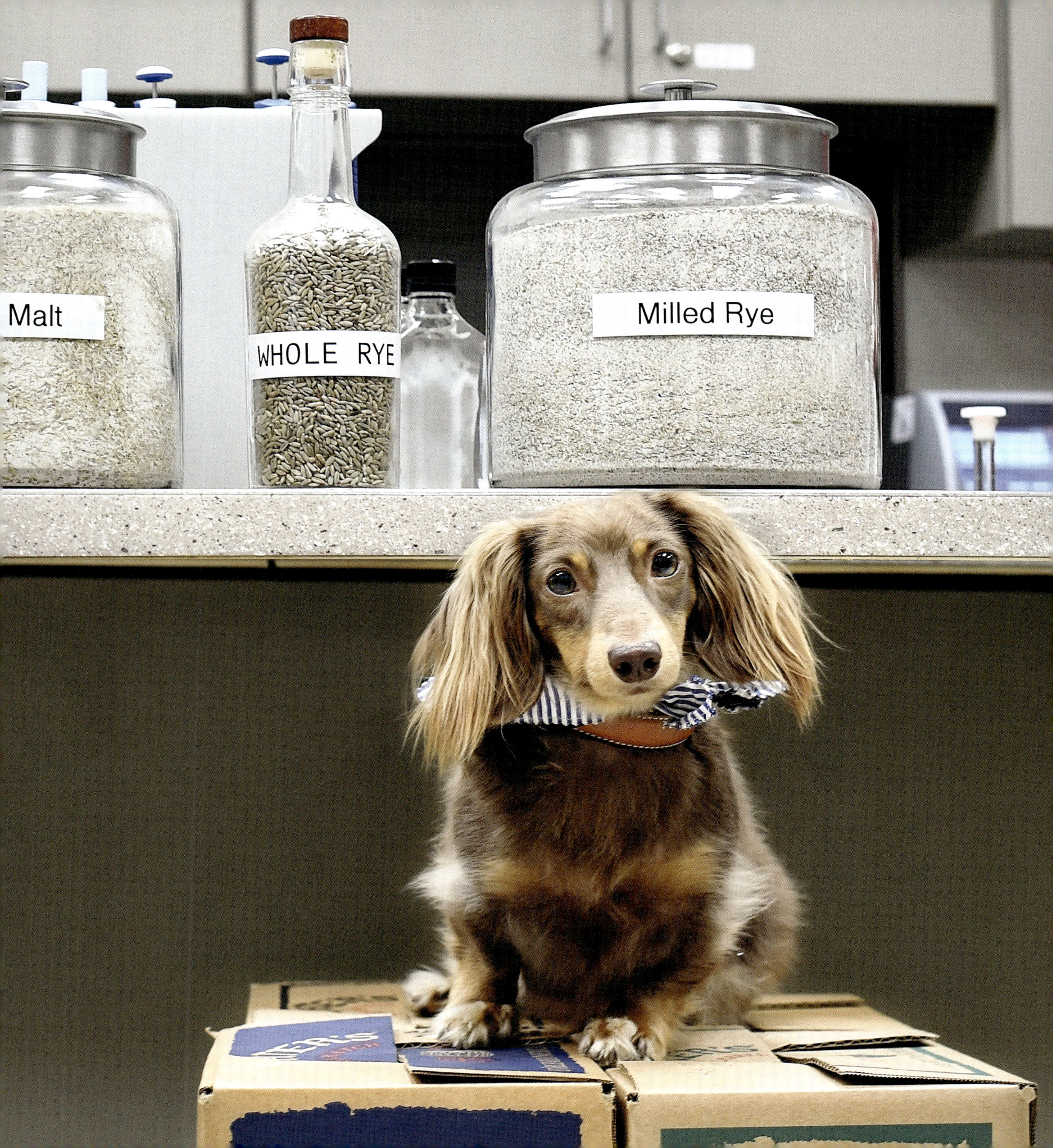
Malt
WHOLE RYE
Milled Rye

WILLOW

Angie Winn

Photographed at Jeptha Creed Distillery

Willow is gentle, mellow, loving and kind-with a good sense of humor. She never barks and is offended by dogs who do. She sits like a person in the car when she travels with her family. She also loves to hang out at the farm with other animals and she loves them all.

Sometimes found: Sleeping curled up next to baby birds

Favorite Places: In the horse barn or in the lake

Reminds her family of: A grandma

PATCHES

Andrea Wilson, Master of Maturation at Michter's Distillery

Patches literally wandered into Andrea's life about 12 years ago. She was lost and they could not locate her family so she became a part of theirs! Andrea says she is thankful every day to have Patches in her life. She is happy, loving, kind and just plain wonderful.

Obsession: Dr. Tim's Chicken Strips

Often Found: Patrolling the backyard

Distillery Buddies: Dan and Norm

ANGO and JACKIE ZYKAN

Jackie Zykan, Master Taster of Old Forester Bourbon

Ango is named after Angostura Bitters, which makes sense since his best friend, Jackie Zykan, is the Master Taster at Old Forester! Jackie adopted Ango from the Kentucky Humane Society and she says that, while she has had many dogs in her life, he is her heart dog and her spirit animal dog. Ango is a big, loving, laid-back guy who is not only a wonderful companion but also a fun partner in life.

Favorite Activity: Hiking and camping

Favorite Treat: Bones

Best Friend: Chi Chi Chicharrone the cat

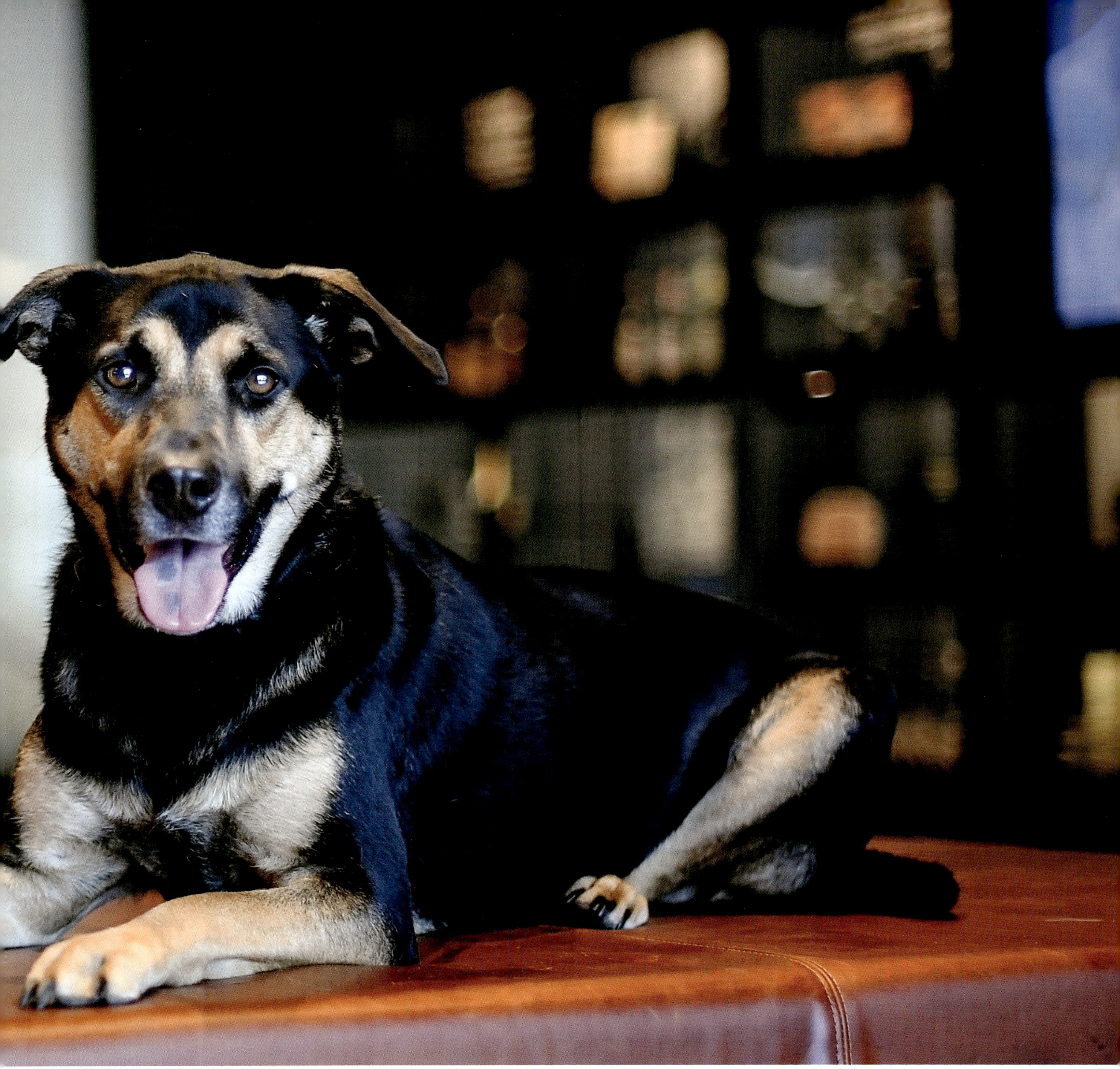

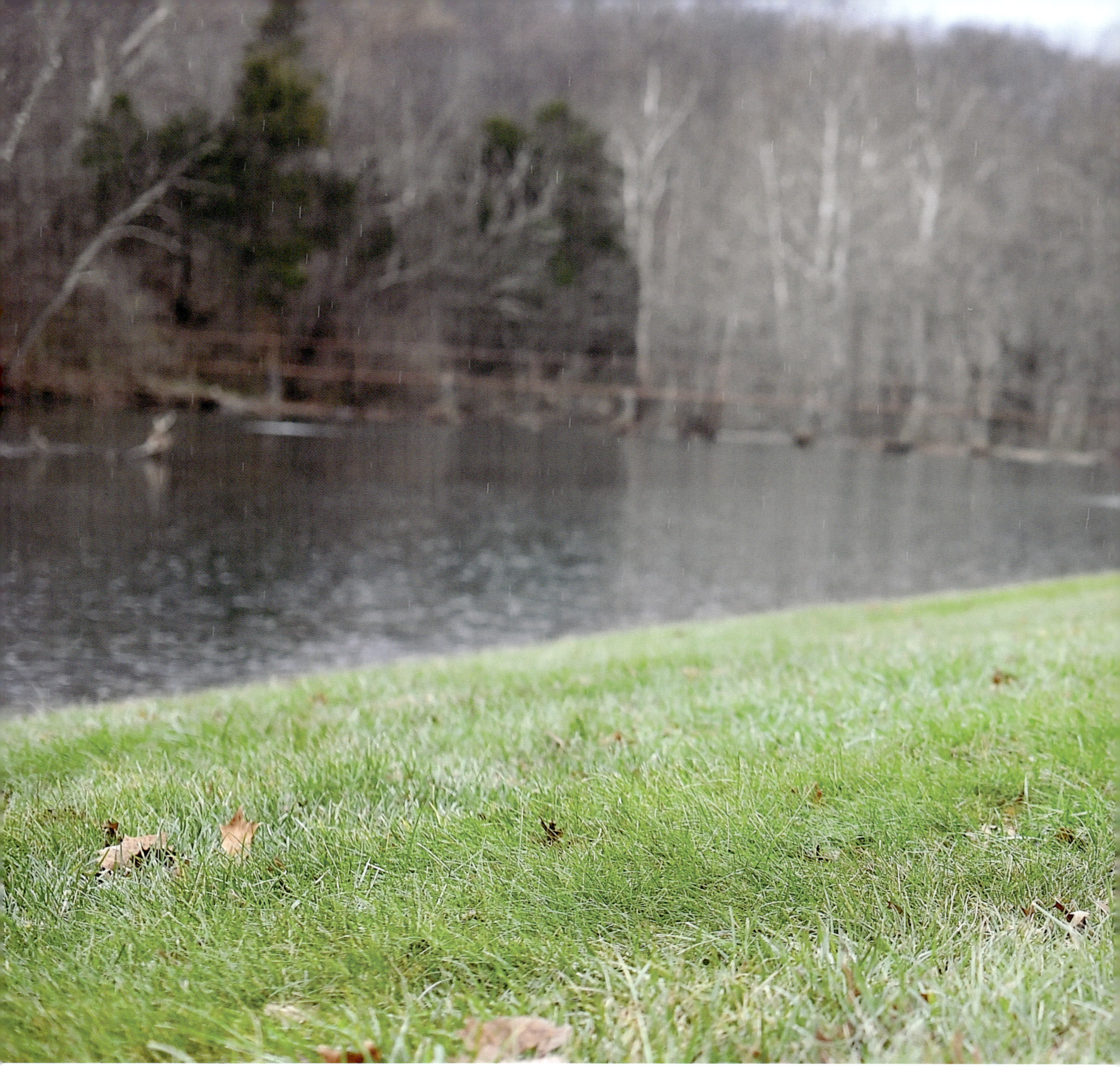

DINGO

Cathy Shircliff

Photographed at The Woodford Reserve Distillery

Dingo comes all the way from the US Virgin Islands. He was tied to a tree for 8 months before he was rescued by his mom and flown to the U.S. for a life of love and cuddles. He's a snuggly little guy who's almost friendly to a fault and animated as any dog could ever be!

Favorite Foods: Apples and cheese

Pet Peeve: Being stuck on a leash when he SHOULD be socializing!

Funniest Trait: His "derpy" ears and smile

LEXINGTON

Ben Drake, Tour Guide at James E. Pepper Distillery

Lexie was adopted from the Lexington Humane Society, which is how she found her name.   She loves field trips, especially to the distillery, and she also loves to play with her sister, Fern.

Usually Found: Shedding
Strangest Habit: Suckling blankets
Favorite Treat: Pigs' ears

LOLA

Melissa Connell, Administrative Assistant at Michter's Distillery

Lola was rescued from a field but has become quite accustomed to the luxuries of life. She now enjoys spending time in the hot tub and loves to give nose cuddles.

Favorite Treat: Peanut butter

Pet Peeve: Forced cuddling

JACKIE

Debra Griffon
Photographed at Maker's Mark Distillery

Jackie is a "petite" 100 pound Great Pyrenees. She was named after her "brother's" stuffed animals at the time, since she was a gift to him when he was five years old. He's now a teenager and his stuffed animals named Jack, Big Jack, and Huge Jack have been completely replaced by Jackie.

Often Found: In the car, ready to ride!
Favorite Place: The couch
Her one bad habit: Barking, which she does loudly and often

JACKIE
Photographed at Maker's Mark Distillery

Buffalo Trace Distillery Golden Biscuit

1 oz. White Dog
1.5 oz. Dr. McGillicuddy's peach Schnapps
1.5 oz. sparkling wine
Dash of ground cinnamon

CHAKAL

Sarah Newman, Events Manager at Buffalo Trace Distillery

Chakal came to live with Sarah after his first family moved back to Turkey. His name actually means "jackal" in Turkish. Chakal, with his big heart and his love for cuddling, is an amazingly gentle and loving dog who has helped Sarah through all the emotional roller coasters of life.

Favorite Activities: Fetching sticks from the water
Proudest Moments: Showing off his new haircuts
Pet Peeve: Sharing the bed or couch with another dog
Favorite Treat: Deli meat

Paws for Thought...
The Angel's Share is the amount of distilled spirits lost to evaporation from the barrel or cask into the air as the whiskey ages. The angels in heaven essentially take their Share of the evaporated bourbon.

"*Who you calling 'bad dog?'" You're the one who told 'the angel's share' story.*"

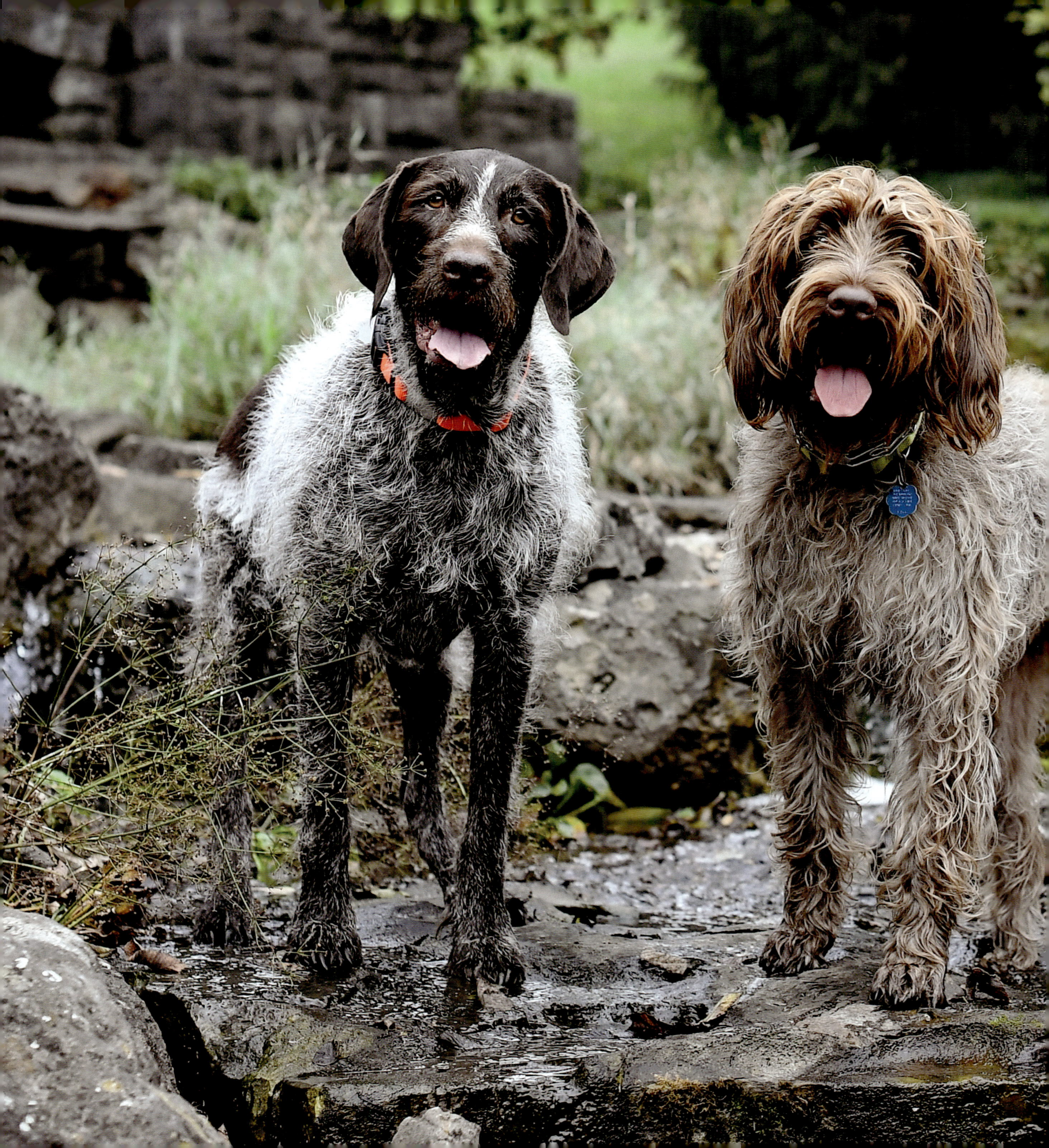

FINNEGAN and WYATT

Gene and Lucy Slusher, Sazerac Events Manager

Photographed at Buffalo Trace Distillery

Finnegan and Wyatt are Wirehaired Pointing Griffons and they love to be outdoors. They are best friends and will run and play all day outside when they have the chance.

FINNEGAN
Pet peeves: Squirrels and trains
Favorite Toy: Tennis balls

WYATT
Best Trait: His goofiness
Favorite Treat: Pigs ears'
Birthday: 4th of July

OSCAR

Jaclyn Poore
Photographed at Jeptha Creed Distillery

Oscar is a quiet and thoughtful little guy. Sometimes it's a little hard to know what he is thinking about, since he spends much of his time standing and staring at the wall. But his family would like to imagine he is planning his next escapade or figuring out how to keep his brother from grabbing his tail! Or maybe he's just soaking up the love of his family, which is vast!

Biggest Dilemma: Can't seem to discern between fingers and treats
Usually Found: With his brother, like it or not
Unusual Skill: Hopping down the steps on his two front feet

FERN

Ben Drake, Tour Guide at James E. Pepper Distillery

Fern was found in the woods by a hiker who brought her to the distillery to find a home for her. Ben took her home and she has been in his family ever since.

Favorite Snack: Olives

Favorite Activity: Running

LUCY

The Davenport Family and Catherine Delaney
Catherine Delaney is Manager of Visitor Experience, The Woodford Reserve Distillery

Lucy is a quiet little dog now, but as a youngster she was never idle. Her favorite activity was to run beside her mom's bike on the Anchorage horse trails: She'd follow along, with that little smiley dog face just as happy as can be.

Nickname: Big Mouth Bass because she circles the coffee table and waits for an opportunity to grab some food

Favorite Stolen Prize: Pizza

Evil Nemesis: Moles

RUBY

Kristen and Andy Shapira
Photographed at Evan Williams Bourbon Experience

Ruby came into the Shapira's home with the important job of curing their daughter of her fear of dogs! She is so sweet, gentle and loving that it took her no time at all to complete her mission.

Favorite Toy: Any one of her many stuffed lambs
Pet Peeve: Hugs
Favorite Activity: Barking at trucks
Favorite Treat: Deer poop-even with hot sauce on it

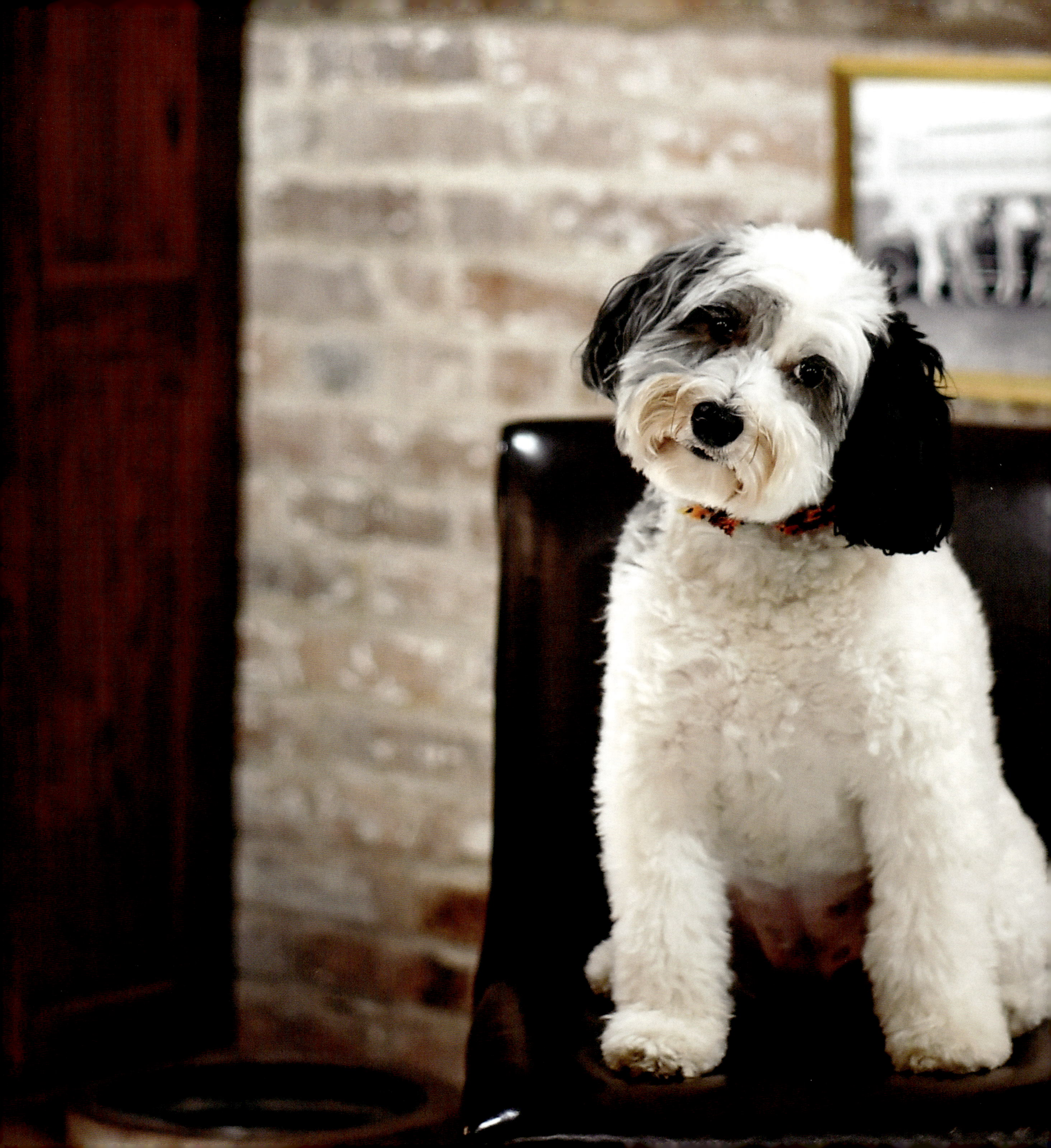

DRINKING ON PREMISE **PROHIBITED** BY ORDER OF THE 18TH AMENDMENT

RUBY
Photographed at Evan Williams Bourbon Experience

WILLOW and NOBLE

Dawn Saul and David Mandell, former President and CEO of Bardstown Bourbon Company

Willow gets away with a lot because she is so completely adorable. She doesn't really care to listen to David and Dawn. She prefers to go her own way and get her own way. But she is such a sweet, irresistible cuddler that it's impossible for them to get too annoyed.

Favorite Activity: Destruction. She especially enjoys ripping apart carpets and turning over tables.

Favorite Food: Frozen blueberries but she is a social eater and will only eat any food if someone sits with her and keeps her company.

Favorite Toy: Cat in the Hat

Noble is the queen of the pack. She can often be found stalking her sister, Willow, or snorting like a piggy. She loves to run around the distillery and when she tires of running, she likes to be held like a baby. If she's really tired she will sleep, most happily when she can burrow under the sheets.

Favorite Activity: Cornhole

Greatest Talent: Singing like a human

Favorite Treat: Raspberry sorbet

The French Toast

Inspired by the Frenchies of Bardstown Bourbon Company

For Man:
1 1/2 oz. Andouille-Washed Bardstown Bourbon Company Collaboration Brandy Finish*
1/2 oz. Louisa's Caramel Pecan Liqueur
1/2 oz. maple syrup
1 egg white

Dry shake vigorously.
Shake on ice.
Strain into large coupe.

For Beast:
1 oz. Andouille-Washed Heavy Cream
1/4 oz. maple syrup
1 egg white

To create the andouille-washed bourbon
Slice 1 lb. andouille.
Warm on low temperature for 15 minutes.
Render out the 2 oz. of fat into 750 ml. of Bardstown Bourbon Company Collaboration Brandy Finish.
Refrigerate for four hours.
Strain off fat solids with a coffee filter.

Dawn Saul with David Mandell, former President and CEO of Bardstown Bourbon Company

Paws for Thought...
A "bourbon flight" is a term used to describe a selection of at least three different types of bourbon. Bourbon flights are usually offered on bar/restaurant menus and commonly offered in one-ounce servings.

"Who ordered the flight of puppies?"

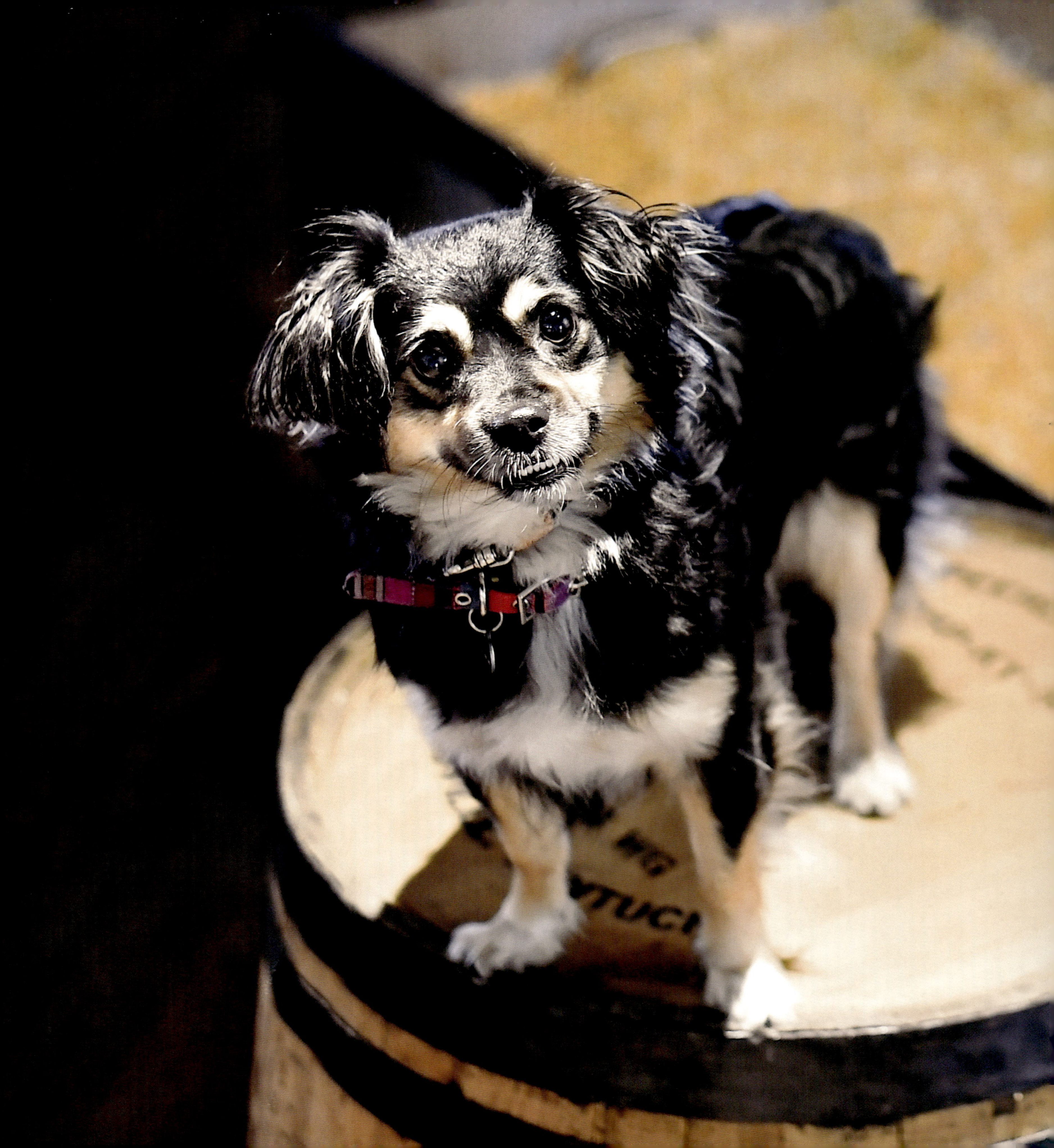

SOOKIE
Photographed at KentuckyPeerless Distilling Company

ROXY

Justin Curl, Mechanic at Brown-Forman

Photographed at Early Times Distillery

Roxy is a mellow girl who loves all of the six children and two cats in her home. She can usually be found sleeping with the cats or being used as a pillow by the children.

Favorite TV Show: Paw Patrol

Best Trick: Playing pony

Pet Peeve: Vacuum cleaners

SUNNY

Lauren Bradley, Brand Specialist at Four Roses Distillery

Adopted from the Franklin County Humane Society, Sunny is a little socialite who loves all people and dogs. She is a beautiful little soul who makes everything better!

Best Trick: Her very fancy routine, which involves turning, sitting, shaking hands and lying down all in a row!

Favorite Activity: Stealing socks and sometimes making a bed out of them!

Favorite Place: In someone's lap

ALPHA
Photographed Angel's Envy Distillery

WES HENDERSON

Wes Henderson, Co-Founder and Chief Innovation Officer of Angel's Envy Distillery has four adopted dogs in his home.

Pictured left to right: Caroline, Jade, Alpha and Bella.

Whether they are catching turtles, climbing trees, chasing squirrels or climbing into home delivery trucks for treats. These furry family members always keep the Hendersons on their toes, and they certainly wouldn't have it any other way.

RUFUS and SOPHIE

Kyle Lloyd, Director Research and Development at Michter's Distillery

Rufus and Sophie are both pug mix rescues who love doing everything together. While they came from separate places, they consider themselves siblings and are sometimes double trouble-especially when it comes to their escapades in the back yard.

Naughty Trick: Expert level hole digging

Favorite Activities: Insect hunting, hiking and sleeping

Favorite Snack: Clementines

SAMMY

Erika Wilhelmi

Photographed at Kentucky Artisan Distillery

Sammy is almost is too cute to be real. He's the life of the party and loves being a socialite with other dogs and people. His mom says he has the power to make everyone happy, enjoy life and, most importantly, live in the present moment.

Often Found: Dragging around one of his toys

Favorite Treat: Butcher Bones

Best Trick: Finding his way into the garbage can, although he's learning that's not the best trick to have!

SAMMY
Photographed at Kentucky Artisan Distillery

ANNABELLE

Becky Przybylak, Heaven Hill Distillery Shipping and Receiving Supervisor

Annabelle is a big girl who loves to chill. She's a Dogue de Bordeaux, a French breed you might recognize from the movie "Turner and Hooch". She is a loyal and loving girl and she loves nothing more than a quiet day at home with her family.

Favorite Toy: A coffee can

Pet Peeve: Outings and photo shoots

LUCIA and JOE MAGLIOCCO

Allison and Joe Magliocco. Joe is President of Michter's Distillery.

When Lucia was rescued she couldn't walk. After five operations on her legs, her mobility greatly improved. But soon after she lost most of her sight and became plagued with digestive issues. Lucia is one of those dogs who teach us to be better and stronger. Despite her physical issues, she is still full of joy every single day. She makes her household complete.

Favorite Toy: Squeaky Pig

Best Talent: Frisbee and ball catching

Oddest Talent: She twerks

Favorite Activity: Presenting her toys as gifts to visitors

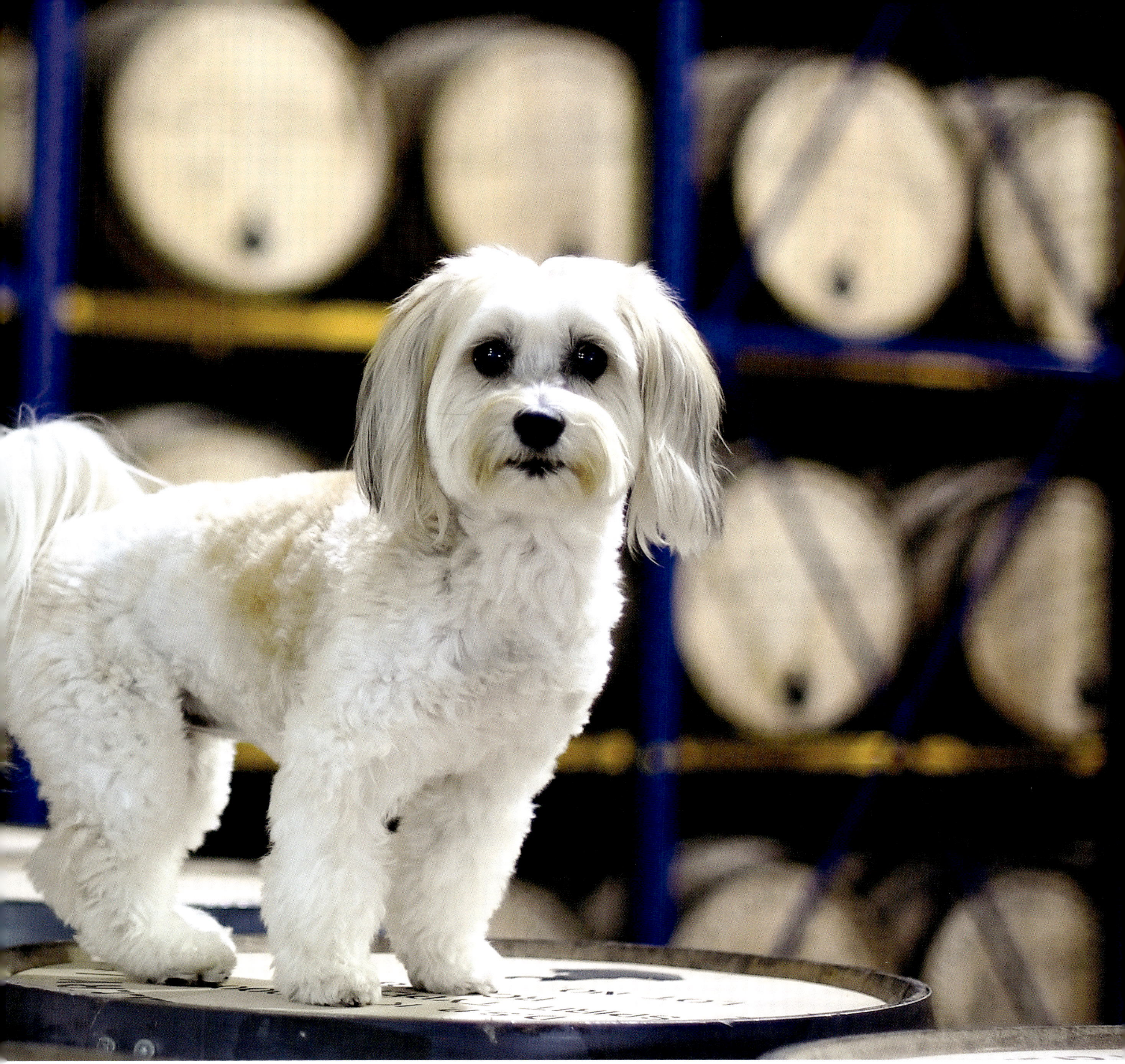

Tess is pictured with Rye, the distillery cat and official greeter.

TESS

Kyle and Peyton Beall, Director of Retail at Kentucky Peerless Distilling Company

Tess is 11 years old. He is wise and wonderful. He has a bit of a serious demeanor, always making sure everyone is well placed and protected. He's often seen looking out the window to be sure nothing is coming to harm the family.

Best Trick: High Fives

Favorite Treat: Peanut butter

Favorite Activity: Playing with brother Jack

TUCKER

Jamie and Corky Taylor, Chairman of Kentucky Peerless Distilling Company

Tucker is a character! He loves life and loves his Aunt Georgia the most of anyone. He does not enjoy sleeping in dog beds, but he does like to tear them up and pee on them to show them who is boss!

Favorite Treat: Beef chewies and popcorn

Favorite Activity: Hanging with his five siblings

Paws for Thought...

For a whiskey to call itself bourbon, its mash, the mixture of grains from which the product is distilled, must contain at least 51% corn.

A guide to Bourbon bottle sizes for dog lovers.

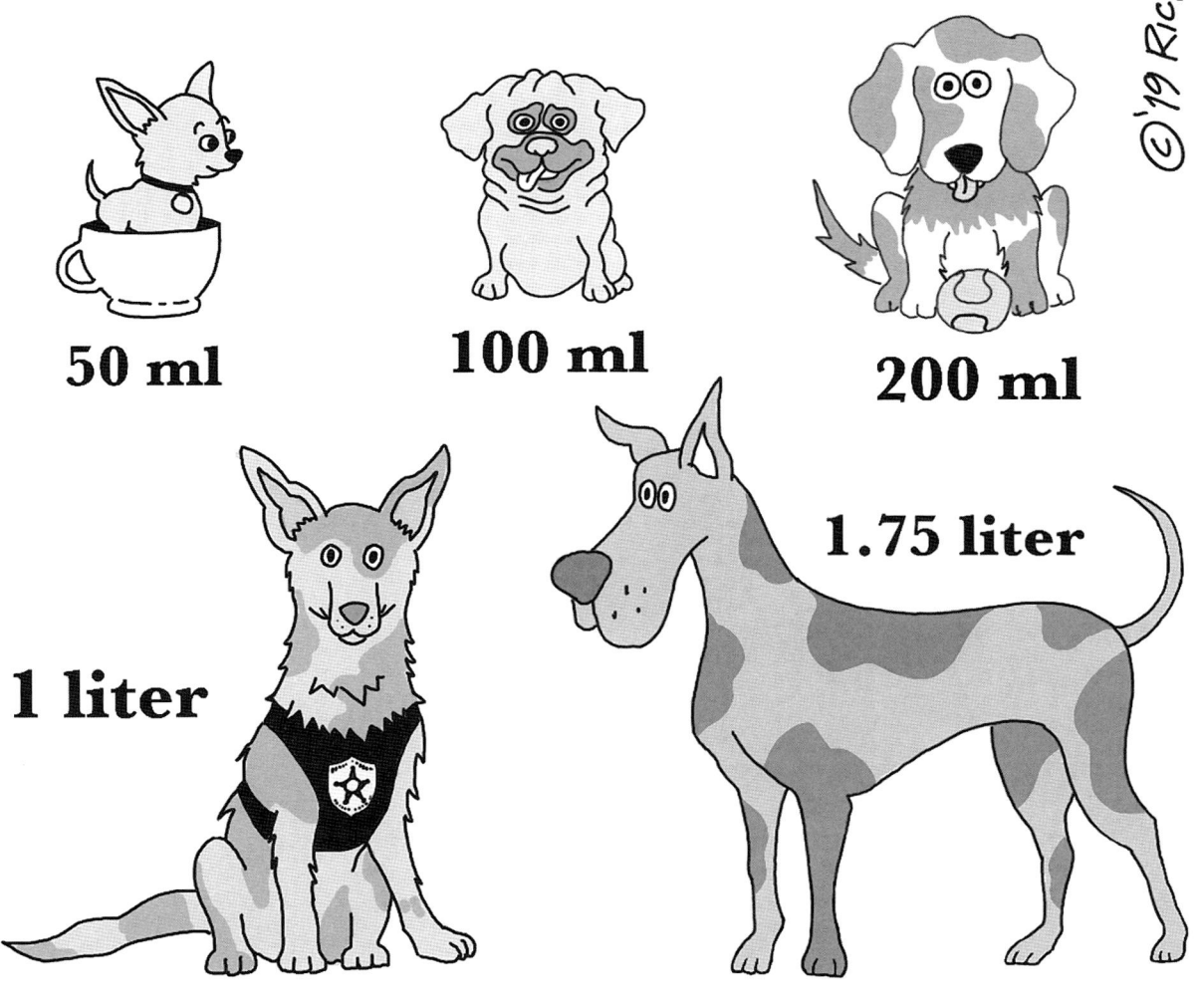

50 ml

100 ml

200 ml

1 liter

1.75 liter

©'19 Rick Maynard

WHISKEY WILLIAM

Photographed at Heaven Hill Distillery

WILLIE

Cathy Shircliff   Photographed at The Woodford Reserve Distillery

Willie is always the best dressed and most popular wherever he goes. His signature look is a bowtie, but he's been known to experiment with a variety of different looks depending on the social situation. He's a true character, with a big and bold personality to match those ears!

Favorite Foods: Carrots, cheese and scrambled eggs

Pet Peeve: When people don't treat him like the prince he is

Favorite Activity: Bossing his brothers around

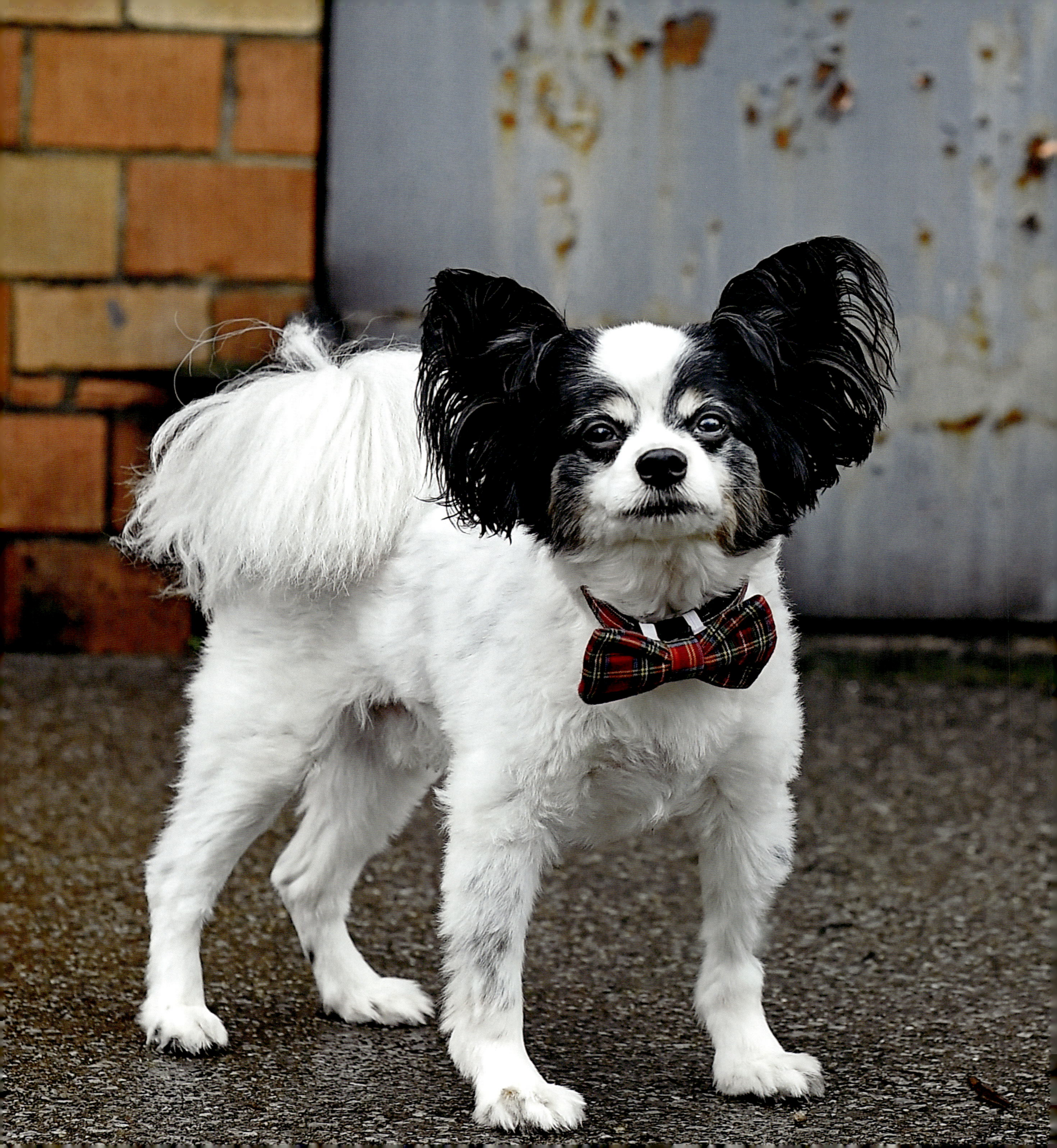

WILLIE
Photographed at The Woodford Reserve Distillery

HILDA

Karla Plott, Mixologist at Evan Williams Bourbon Experience

Hilda is definitely one of the cool kids! She has her own Instagram account and is an award winner, placing first in the Heaven Hill Snuggle Champion Contest! She is sweet, goofy, loyal and an all-around fantastic girl.

Favorite Treat: Egg yolks
Best Friend: His cat sister, Malice
Most Endearing Trick: Bringing gifts to his parents when they get home from work
Favorite Activity: Chasing squirrels

The Milk Bone

1.25 oz. organic peanut butter washed Evan Williams Black Label
1/3 cup organic whole milk
1 teaspoon organic vanilla bean paste
1 pint of premium organic vanilla ice cream

Blend until desired smoothness.

Top with browned butter, crushed organic graham cracker, and candied bacon strip for garnish.

To wash bourbon with peanut butter:
Add 1 cup smooth organic peanut butter into a clean mason jar.

Add one 750 ml of Evan Williams Black Label.

Use long spoon to mix together.

Close lid and gently shake.

Store 24-48 hours in a cool, dark place shaking every 12 hours until desired flavor is achieved.

Strain off bourbon with mesh strainer or cheesecloth.

To reduce prep time, add a tablespoon of peanut butter and 1.25 of regular Evan Williams Signature Black Label.

BOO
Photographed at Jeptha Creed Distillery

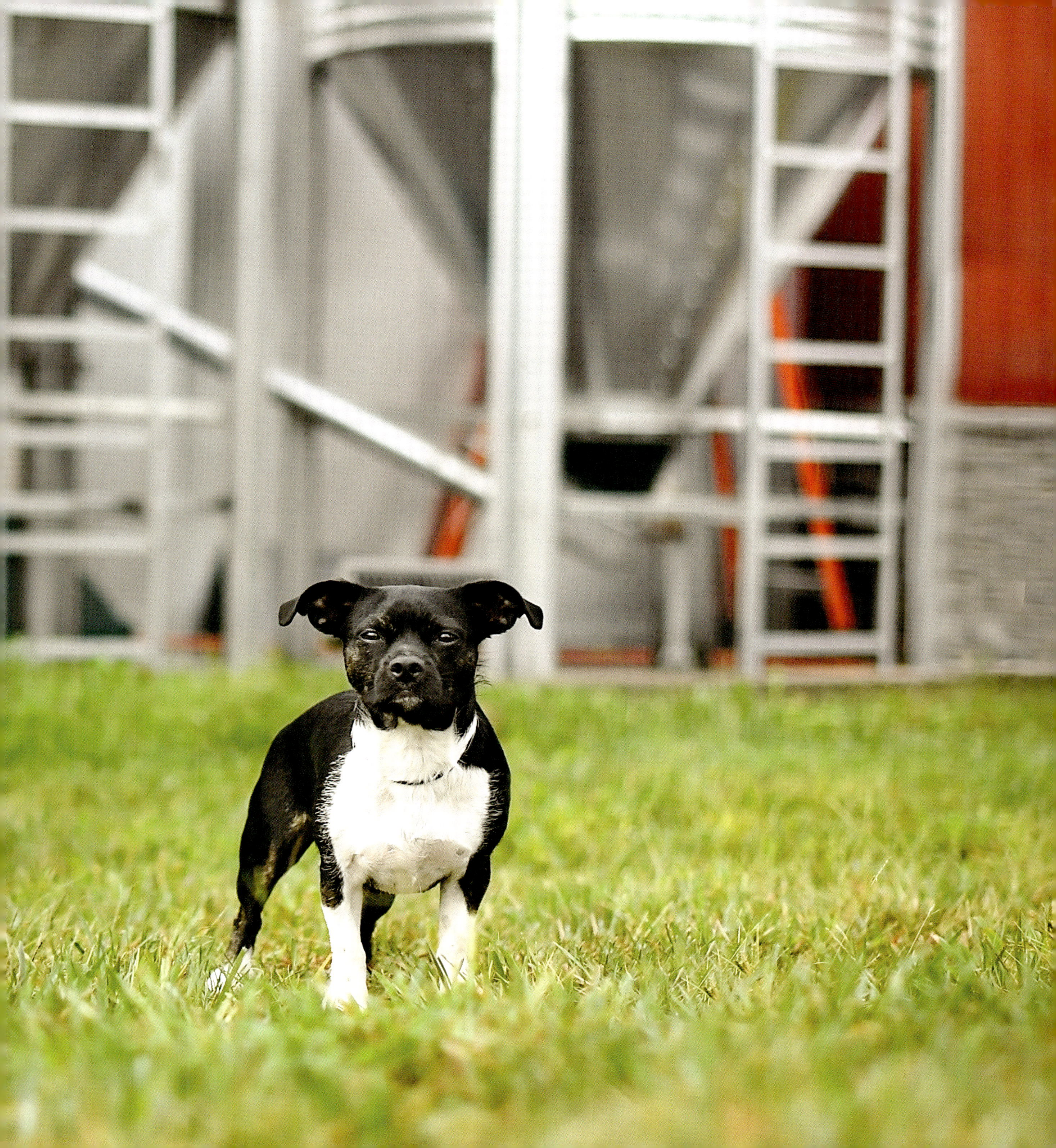

STORM

Andrew Henderson, Lead Distiller at Angel's Envy Distillery

Storm is so loving he must constantly be in physical contact with either Andrew or his wife, Sarah. This can be a little annoying when he is chewing bones, but most of the time it's very endearing. He can't go up or down the stairs without a chew toy or bone and if he can't find one, he runs around the house until he does so he can proceed to the steps.

Favorite Foods: Scrambled eggs and peanut butter bones

Favorite Activity: Jogging with his family

RED

Steve Thompson (1942 - 2021), President and Majority owner of Kentucky Artisan Distillery

Red is adopted from a golden retriever rescue that saved him from a life where he was caged all the time. Steve originally wanted a watchdog but Red is the opposite and runs to greet strangers rather than barking at them! He's 100% happy in the wonderful life he deserves!

Favorite Activity: Eating

Favorite foods to eat: Hotdogs and jerky

MILLIE and MACY

Cordell Lawrence, Director of Global Marketing and Strategy for Kentucky Peerless Distilling Company

Millie and Macy are an adorable pair that are truly the dynamic duo. Macy is a free spirited troublemaker who craves attention all the time! Millie is much more laid back and loves every person and every dog she meets.

Usually Found: Together-plotting an escape from the fenced yard

Favorite Treats: Baby carrots and Greenies

LULU

Rhoneé Rodgers, Environmental Health Safety Manager at Heaven Hill Distillery

Lulu is a little diva, to be sure. She is all about her family first and loves rubs more than anything. She is almost always happy, but birthdays and Christmas are her favorite times because she loves to open everyone's presents. A lot of times, those presents are for her because she does appreciate a good toy!

Favorite Toy: Peppa Pig

Pet Peeve: Squirrels and rabbits

Best Friend: Aunt Princess

Paws for Thought...

Kentucky's limestone water is very important to making bourbon. The iron is filtered out of the water as it flows over the rock and, as a result, the water becomes a sweet-tasting mineral water.

"Yum. This has to be fresh Bluegrass spring water filtered through a layer of limestone."

MADDIE and OLIVER

Sarah and David Newnan

Photographed at Buffalo Trace Distillery

Maddie and Oliver were both rescued; Maddie from Bluegrass Greyhound Rescue and Oliver was found as a stray on a farm. They are both so grateful for their wonderful lives and try very hard to always be good dogs.

MADDIE:

Best Trick: Hiding an entire bowl of food to eat later when nobody is watching

Favorite Activity: Gathering toys to hoard and keep away from her brother

OLIVER:

Favorite Toy: His giant stuffed duck
Favorite Activity: Chillin'

HAMPDEN and SYDNEY

Betsy Bulleit, photographed at Bulleit Bourbon Distillery

Hampden and Sydney are a loveable brother and sister pair of corgis. Their legs may be short, but their personalities are huge. Their nicknames say everything about their personalities. Hampden is "Mr. Dotodo" because he is so laid back. But he never misses an opportunity to challenge his sister to a good game of chase, even though he always loses. Sydney's nickname is "MeMe" because it's all about her! She is quick and smart and loves to chase balls. Corgis have been a huge part of the Bulleit's lives for a long time. Betsy says if they are good enough for the Queen of England, they are good enough for her, too!

DOTTIE JANE
Photographed at Michter's Distillery

CHASE

Melissa Horton, Corporate Events Manager at Heaven Hill Distillery

Chase is a very energetic and happy boy. He sleeps in the bed but once he's awake, he is a man on the go. He grew up quickly, which still confuses him a bit as he doesn't realize his size. This results in a lot of running into things and trying to fit into spaces too small.

Cutest Skill: Frolicking
Best Skill: Keep away
Favorite Toy: His glow in the dark ball

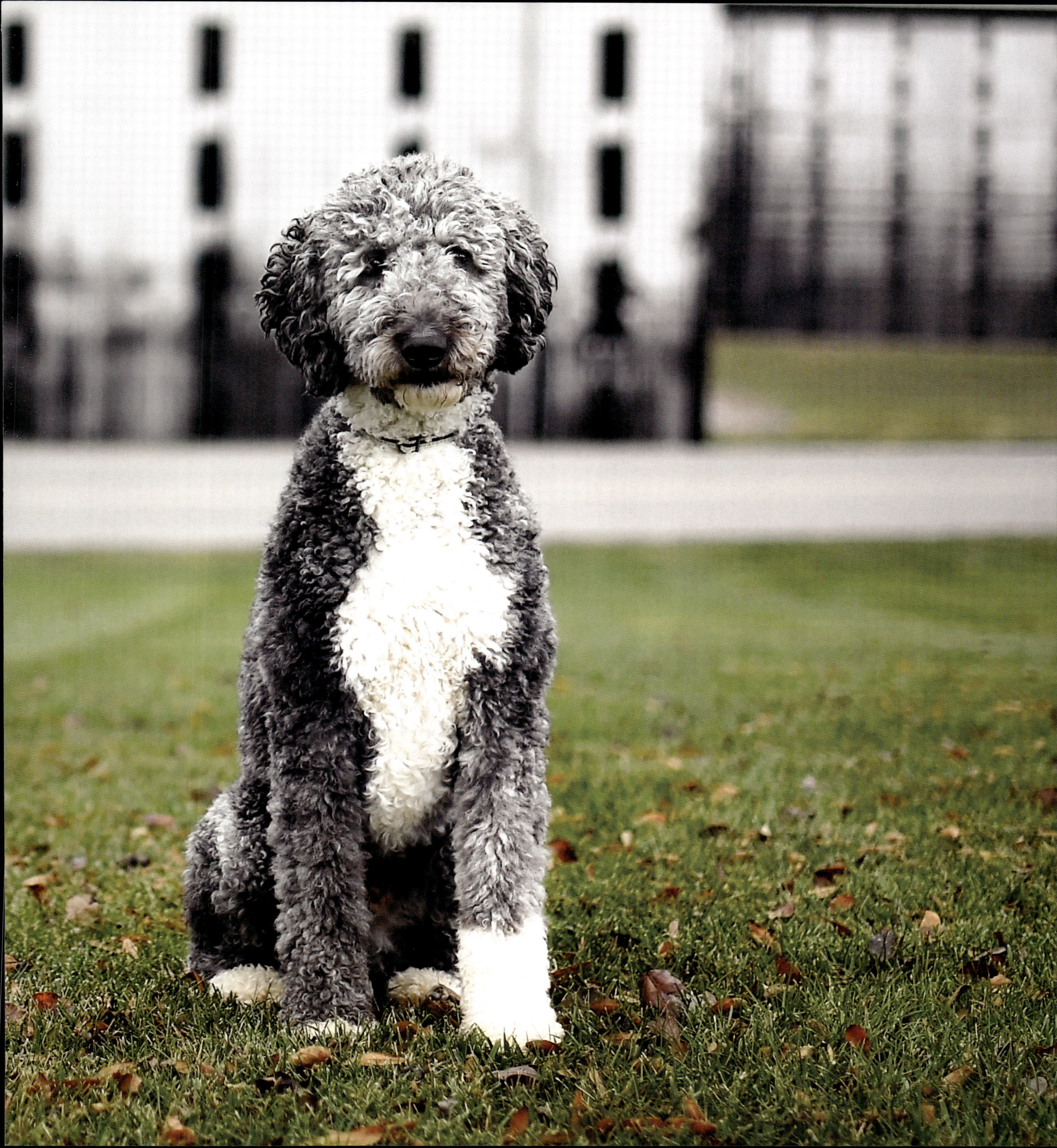

MAGGIE

Ryan Ashley, COO and Director of Distillery Operations at Four Roses Distillery

Maggie is an Anatolian Shepherd/Boxer mix who was adopted as a puppy. She shows unconditional love for her family, but also takes her role as "protector of the realm" very seriously. She is literally a hair bomb, shedding all year around. But her wonderful personality and loyalty make the vacuuming and brushing well worth it!

Funny Quirk: She talks when it's time to go to bed, eat, go for a walk, or go on rides

Worst Habit: Digging "fox holes" in the yard to get the moles

Often Found: Sleeping like a pretzel

Nutty Mutthatton

1½ fl. oz. Four Roses Small Batch
1 fl .oz. sweet vermouth
2 dashes black walnut bitters
Cherry

We recommend Carpano Antica vermouth for this cocktail.

Add bourbon, vermouth, bitters and ice to mixing glass. Stir until glass is frosted.

Use strainer to separate ice and cocktails into chilled martini glass (neat). Add cherry. Stir.

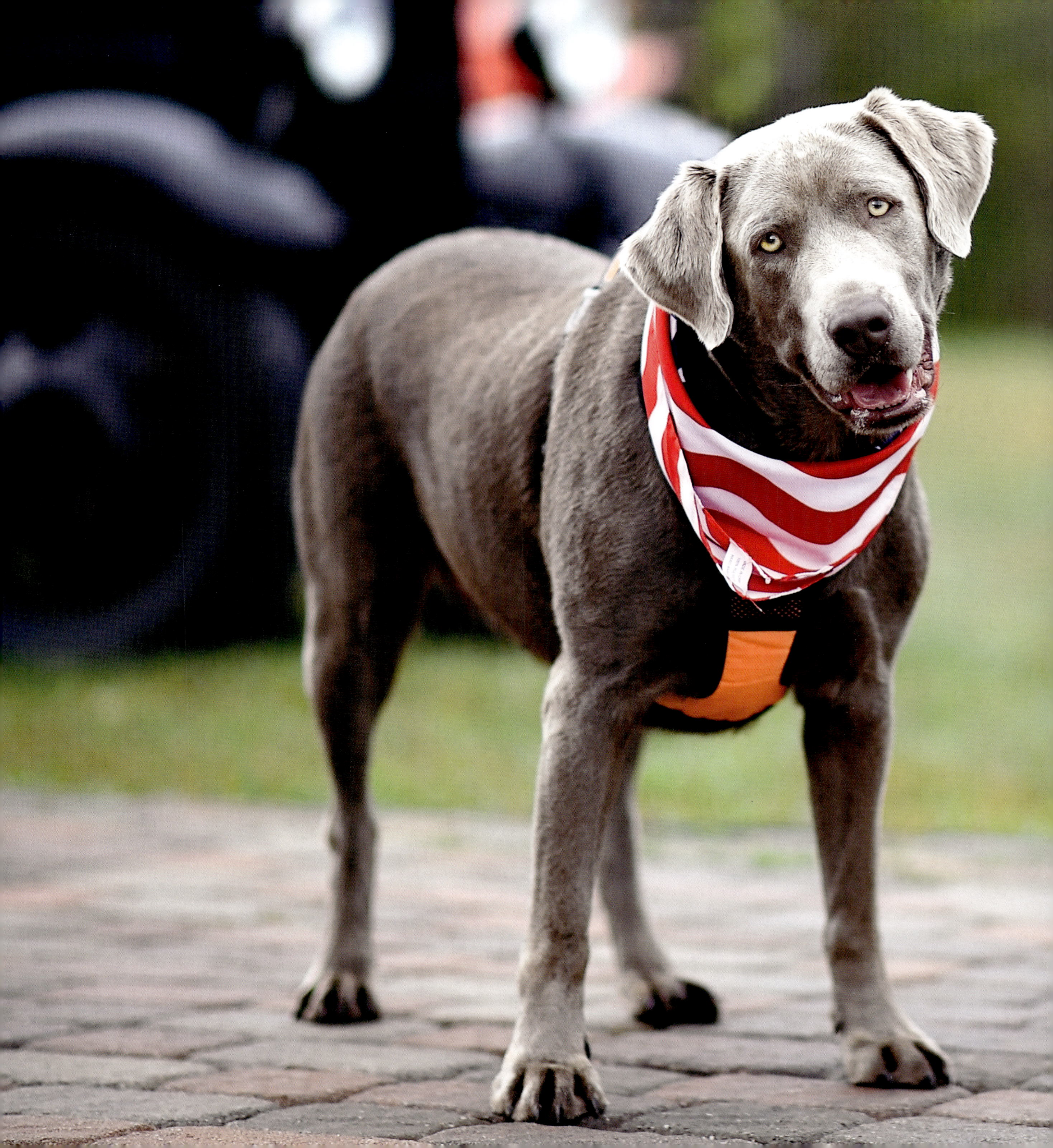

BRANDY
Photographed at Jeptha Creed Distillery

ZOE

Bill Waddell

Photographed at Kentucky Peerless Distilling Company

When Zoe is not tending bar, she prides herself on being the boxer who is always dressed for success. Her favorite accessory is her life jacket, which she uses to swim in the lake. She also enjoys a variety of coats and other outerwear to make sure she is prepared for whatever Mother Nature brings.

Favorite Activity: Beach digging in the sand

Favorite Treat: Anything edible

Best Friends: A family of deer because she thinks she is one of them.